Welcome to Japan

Japan

By Elma Schemenauer

The Child's World®

Published by The Child's World®
1980 Lookout Drive
Mankato, MN 56003-1705
800-599-READ
www.childsworld.com

Content Adviser: Alisa Freedman, Assistant Professor of Japanese Literature and Film,
Department of East Asian Languages and Literatures, University of Oregon, Eugene, OR

Design and Production: The Creative Spark, San Juan Capistrano, CA

Editorial: Publisher's Diner, Wendy Mead, Greenwich, CT

Photo Research: Deborah Goodsite, Califon, NJ

Cover and title page: Alan Becker/The Image Bank/Getty Images
Interior photos: Alamy: 6 (Jtb Photo Communications, Inc.), 13 (Jon Arnold Images), 22 (Jeremy
Sutton-Hibbert), 27 (Jon Arnold Images); AP Photo: 26 (Itsuo Inouye); Corbis: 16 inset (Karen
Kasmauski); Dreamstime.com: 31 (Chase Leland); Getty Images: 17 (Paul Chesley/National
Geographic), 23 (Nick Clements/Taxi); iStockphoto.com: 8 (Anna Dzondzua), 28 (Ufuk Zivana);
Landov: 20 left (Haruyoshi Yanaguchi/Bloomberg News), 29 (Tomohiro Ohsumi/Bloomberg News);
Lonely Planet Images: 20 right (Cheryl Forbes), 24 (John Ashburne), 30 (John Hay); Minden Pictures:
3, 9 (Konrad Wothe); NASA Earth Observatory: 4 (Reto Stockli); Oxford Scientific: 7 (Ball Miwako/
Imagestate Ltd), 11 (Jtb Photo Communications Inc), 12 (Rita Ariyoshi/Pacific Stock), 15 (R. Mcleod/
Robert Harding Picture Library Ltd), 3, 16 (Bibikow Walter/Index Stock Imagery), 18 (Gary Conner/
Index Stock Imagery), 21 (Gavin Hellier/Robert Harding Picture Library Ltd), 3, 25 (Aflo Foto Agency);
Panos Pictures: 14 (Mark Henley), 19 (Toru Morimoto); SuperStock: 10 (age fotostock).
Map: XNR Productions: 5

Library of Congress Cataloging-in-Publication Data
Schemenauer, Elma.
  Welcome to Japan / by Elma Schemenauer.
    p. cm. — (Welcome to the world)
  Includes index.
  ISBN-13: 978-1-59296-913-5 (library bound : alk. paper)
  ISBN-10: 1-59296-913-5 (library bound : alk. paper)
  1. Japan—Juvenile literature. I. Title.
DS806.S365 2007
952—dc22
                                        2007006196

Welcome to the WORLD

Contents

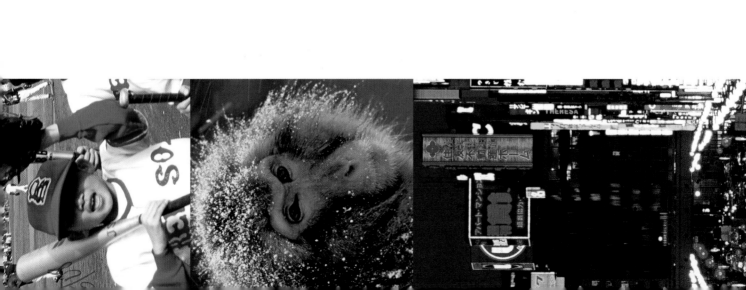

Where Is Japan?

If you could look down on Earth from high above, you would see large land areas surrounded by water. These land areas are called **continents**. Some continents are made up of several different countries. Japan is an island country off the continent of Asia. Japan is a beautiful country that's full of interesting people and places.

This picture gives us a flat look at Earth. Japan can be found inside the red circle.

Did you know?

Japan is made up of four big islands and thousands of smaller ones.

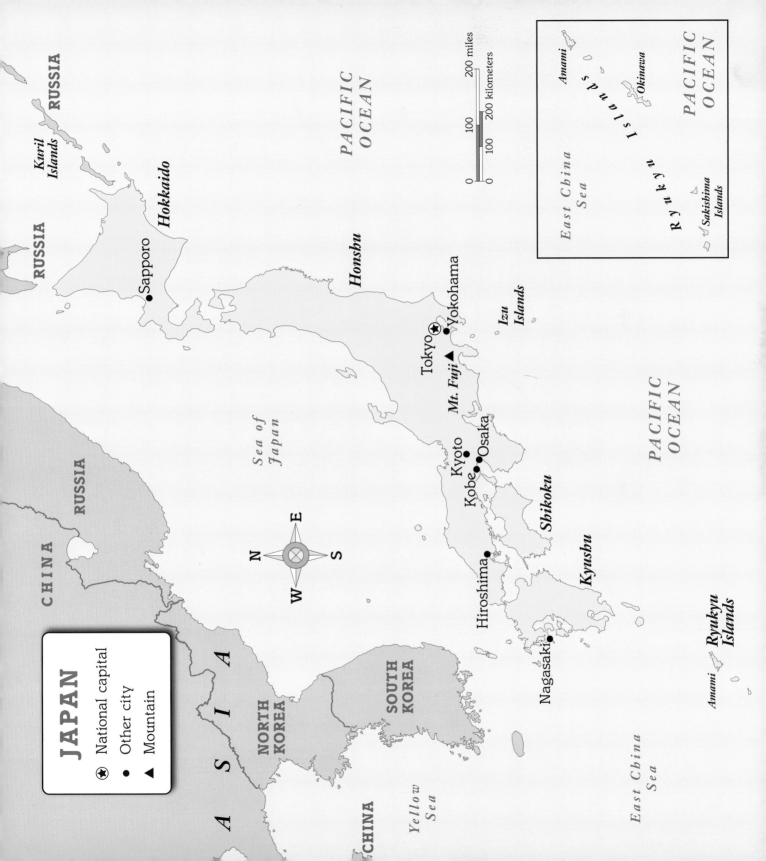

The Land

Most countries are made up of one piece of land. But not Japan! Japan is made up of thousands of islands. The islands were formed long ago when huge volcanoes erupted under the ocean. Hot melted rock called **lava** spilled out underwater. When the lava cooled, it hardened to form the islands.

Most of Japan's islands are very small. Only four of the islands are big enough for people to build cities on.

Rebun Island is one of the many islands that make up the country of Japan.

Mount Fuji

Hokkaido (ho-ky-doh) is a big island in the northern part of Japan. It is covered with mountains and forests. The island of Honshu (hone-shoo) has Japan's highest mountain. It is called Mount Fuji. The island of Shikoku (shi-ko-koo) gets lots of rain. Kyushu (kyoo-shoo) has the warmest weather of all Japan's islands.

Did you know?

Japan is a country that has a lot of earthquakes. Every year there are about 1,500 small earthquakes, or tremors, all over the country.

Plants and Animals

Each area of Japan has different plants and animals. Bears and deer live in the forests of Hokkaido. On the island of Honshu, people who go hiking sometimes see eagles. Some areas of Japan have beautiful cherry trees for people to enjoy. In the mountains, people can see red-faced Japanese monkeys. These monkeys are known as **macaques** (muh-KAKS). Macaques are also called snow monkeys because they live in colder areas.

Did you know?

Many Japanese people raise bonsai (bon-siy) trees. The trees are very small and are grown in pots. Many people like to trim and shape their bonsai trees so they look different from everyone else's.

With its thick fur, this macaque does not mind the cold weather.

Thousands of years ago, Hokkaido was connected to Asia by a land bridge. Researchers believe that a second bridge may have linked Kyushu to what is now South Korea.

The land bridges may have disappeared, but today lots of human-made bridges can be found in Japan.

Long Ago

The first people came to Japan about 18,000 years ago. But how did they get there? Long ago, the oceans weren't as deep as they are now. Much of the world's water was frozen into ice. In some places, pieces of land connected the continents together. These pieces of land are called **land bridges.** People could walk from one continent to another without having to cross the ocean. They just walked across the ice.

Over time, the ground slowly warmed up. The ice melted and water covered up the bridges. The people who had walked to Japan had to stay. That is how people came to Japan's islands.

Japan Today

Emperors once lived here in Kumamoto castle.

For a long time, Japan has been ruled by **emperors**. An emperor had a lot of power over the people. Today, Japan's emperor is not very powerful. He does not make rules for the country anymore. Instead, Japan's laws are made by its **parliament**. The people in Japan's parliament talk about how their country is doing. They make laws to keep the Japanese people safe. They also think of ways to make Japan a better place to live.

The Japanese parliament building in Tokyo

The People

About 127 million people live in Japan. Most of them live near the coasts of the big islands. If you visited Japan, you would see mostly Japanese faces around you. That's because in Japan, almost everyone is Japanese.

Manners are very important in Japan. Japanese people believe in being polite and treating others with respect. They try to help each other and be good neighbors. Being kind to other people is a very old and important part of Japanese life.

Many people live in Tokyo, Japan's capital city.

People shop for food at a local market.

Japan's big cities are usually crowded, busy places. Space is very limited so people often have small apartments.

Farmers on Honshu

City Life and Country Life

In Japan, almost everyone lives in cities. The biggest city is Tokyo (toh-kyoh) on the island of Honshu. Most city families live in apartments. These apartments are very small. That's because Japan's cities are very crowded! In Japan's cities, families must learn ways to save space.

Out in the country, there aren't as many people. Many Japanese country-dwellers live in wooden houses. Usually, these houses are in towns. Some families live on farms. Country people try to help their neighbors and be good friends.

Did you know?

The shinkansen (shin-kahn-sen), or "Bullet Train," is a special train in Japan. It is one of the fastest trains in the world—it can go up to 160 miles per hour!

17

Schools and Language

A student works on his math homework.

Japanese children start school when they are six years old. They learn math and social studies just as you do. Japanese students also study art, music, and computers. In the upper grades, Japanese children learn how to speak another language—English. Japanese children work very hard. They even go to school on Saturday mornings.

Japanese children learn two alphabets. And they need to learn about 2,000 characters! These characters are symbols that stand for sounds or words. It takes that many characters to write in Japanese. Japanese is not an easy language, but it is very interesting. Writing some Japanese words is like drawing pictures. And when you speak some Japanese words, they sound just like what they mean. For example, ki-ki (kee-kee) means "squeaky," and goro-goro means "rumbling."

Work

In the cities, people work at all kinds of jobs. Some people work in stores or banks. Others work in offices, hotels, and hospitals. Many others work inside huge factories. There they make things such as cameras, computers, and cars.

In the country, Japanese people have other jobs to do. Many people catch fish. Others make boards and paper from

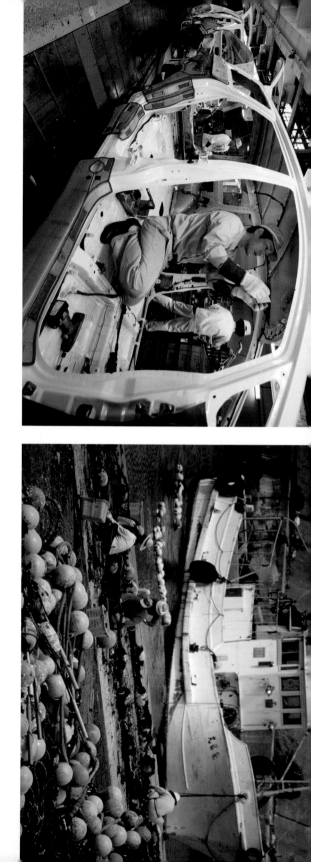

trees. Many other people grow crops such as soybeans, rice, tangerines, and apples. There are also people who work at small shops and restaurants.

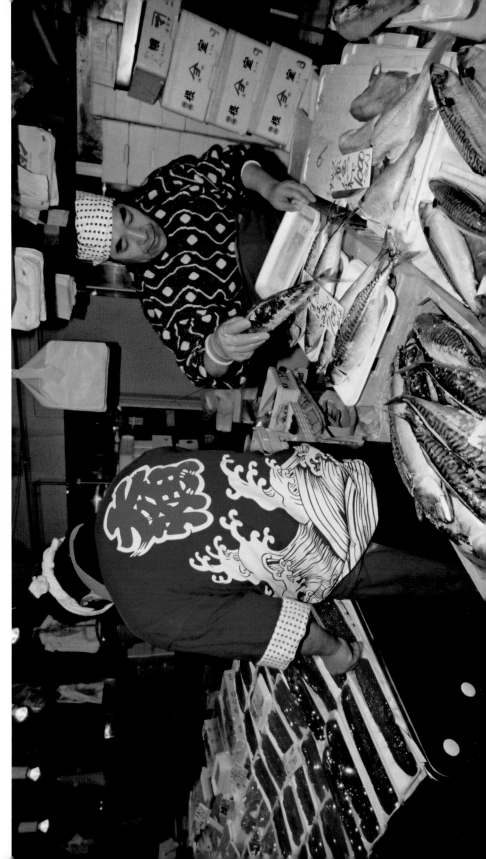

Workers at a fish market in Asahikawa

A family has dinner together at a restaurant.

Food

Japanese people like to eat different kinds of food. They eat lots of rice and vegetables. They also like to eat spinach, mushrooms, and a kind of radish called a daikon (dy-kohn). Sushi (soo-shee) is a very popular dish. It is made of fish and rice. People in Japan eat and cook with special sticks called **chopsticks.** They hold two chopsticks in one hand and use them to pick up food.

Japanese people like to drink tea. It is served everywhere—in restaurants, in offices, and in homes. Japanese tea is pale green or brown. It is served plain, without sugar, milk, or lemon.

A boy has tea with his grandfather.

Pastimes

Judo, karate, and video games were all invented in Japan! People in Japan also play baseball, volleyball, tennis, and golf. Another popular Japanese sport is sumo (soo-mo) wrestling. The art of paper folding—called origami (or-i-gah-mee)—is a popular hobby.

Many Japanese children enjoy watching television and playing computer games just like you. They also read books, magazines, and comic books called manga (man-guh). Some restaurants have stacks of manga for grown-ups to read while they wait for their meals.

Two boys take a break outside to read comics.

These Japanese baseball players pose for a group photograph.

Holidays

Cherry Blossom Festival

Japan has many different holidays. November 15 is the 7-5-3 Festival. On that day, Japanese children who are 7, 5, or 3 years old get to put on special robes called **kimonos.** Kimonos are worn only on special days. The Cherry Blossom Festival comes when the cherry trees bloom.

Families picnic under the cherry trees and look at the beautiful blossoms.

The people of Japan mix the old ways with the new. In Japan you will see a hamburger restaurant next to a Japanese tea room. Children wear blue jeans every day, but for holidays they wear their special kimonos. Japan is a wonderful place to learn about mixing old and new ways together.

Cherry Blossom Festival

Two girls enjoy a laugh together during of the 7-5-3 Festival.

Fast Facts About Japan

Area: About 145,868 square miles (380,000 square kilometers). That is about the size of California.

Population: 127 million people.

Capital City: Tokyo.

Other Important Cities: Hiroshima, Kyoto, Osaka, and Nagasaki.

Money: The yen.

National Holiday: Birthday of the Emperor on December 23.

National Flag: A red circle surrounded by white. The red circle represents the beautiful sun that shines on Japan.

Head of the Government: The prime minister.

Emperor: His Majesty Emperor Akihito.

Famous People:

Takuya Kimura: popular actor and singer

Takeshi Kitano: actor, author, filmmaker

Masatoshi Koshiba: Nobel Prize-winning physicist

Daisuke Matsuzaka: baseball pitcher

Yukio Mishima: famous writer

Hidetoshi Nakata: soccer player

Ryoji Noyori: Nobel Prize-winning chemist

Kenzaburo Oe: Nobel Prize-winning author

Takanohana: professional sumo wrestler

His Majesty Emperor Akihito

National Song: "Kimigayo" (The Reign of Our Emperor)

Ten thousand years of happy reign be thine:
Rule on, my lord, till what are pebbles now
By ages united to mighty rocks shall grow
Whose venerable sides the moss doth line.

Japanese Folklore:

Momotaro: The Peach Boy

There once was an old man and an old woman living in the countryside. Each day they would do their chores. The man who cut wood and the woman would wash their clothes in the river. One day while washing clothes, she noticed a peach floating in the water. She took the peach home. When she cut it open, she discovered a small boy inside. The couple named him Momotaro, or Peach Boy, and raised him as their own child.

Momotaro grew up to be a strong young man. One day he decided that he would go to Ogre Island to get rid of the mean ogres living there. Along the way, Momotaro met a monkey, a dog, and a bird, and they joined him on his quest. When he finally faced the ogres, he was helped by each of his new friends to defeat the ogres.

How Do You Say...

ENGLISH	JAPANESE	HOW TO SAY IT
hello	konnichiwa	koh-nee-che-wah
goodbye	sayonara	sy-oh-nah-ruh
please	onegaishimasu	oh-ne-guy-she-mah-soo
thank you	arigato	ah-ree-gah-toh
one	ichi	ee-chee
two	nii	nee
three	sun	sun
Japan	Nihon	nee-hohn

Glossary

chopsticks (CHOP-stiks) Chopsticks are special sticks that Japanese people use for eating. Two chopsticks are used to pinch food or scoop it up.

continents (KON-tuh-nents) Continents are huge areas of land. Most of the continents are separated by oceans.

emperors (EM-per-rerz) Emperors are rulers, like kings. Japan's emperor was once very powerful.

kimonos (kih-MO-noz) Kimonos are long robes with wide sleeves. Japanese people wear kimonos on special days.

land bridges (LAND BRI-jez) Land bridges were narrow pieces of land that connected the continents long ago. People first came to Japan by walking across land bridges.

lava (LAH-vuh) Lava is hot, melted rock that comes from deep inside Earth. Japan's islands are made of lava.

macaques (muh-KAKS) Macaques are a type of monkey that live in Japan. They are also called snow monkeys.

parliament (PAR-lu-ment) A parliament is a group of government officials that make laws. Japan has a parliament in Tokyo.

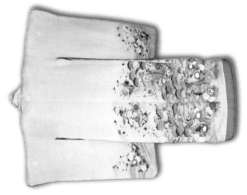

Further Information

Read It

Barber, Nicola. *Tokyo.* Milwaukee, WI: World Almanac Library, 2004.

Harvey, Miles. *Look What Came from Japan.* Danbury, CT: Franklin Watts, 1999.

Nisimura, Shigeo. *An Illustrated History of Japan.* North Clarendon, VT: Tuttle Publishing, 2005.

Look It Up

Visit our Web page for lots of links about Japan:
http://www.childsworld.com/links

Note to Parents, Teachers, and Librarians: We routinely verify our Web links to make sure they are safe, active sites—so encourage your readers to check them out!

Index